AF487991

Coaching Baseball

Coaching Baseball

Larry Geigle

COACHBEAR
BOOKS

ISBN: Hardcover   979-8-218-23806-3
               Softcover   979-8-218-23495-9
               eBook   979-8-218-23496-6

Contents

Introduction to Coaching BaseBall

I promised to write a baseball book for my grandson Logan. Being a retired baseball coach and grandfather, I wanted Logan to know how much I enjoyed watching him go to the plate and smack one over the fence. It was fun to watch all the players cheer each other on. Everyone loved Logan because he played with such a carefree demeanor and didn't get too caught up in the game. To him, it was all about having fun with his friends and being part of a team. His friendships were always more important than baseball. Whether he was on the pitcher's mound or standing at the plate, he always had a smile and gave us reason to cheer. Logan would stand at the plate like a young Babe Ruth and swing his bat with power and precision like the great Bambino did back in the day; at least that's the way Grampa saw it. I think Logan acquired his hitting power from eating pizza and hot dogs during and after the games. Now years later, the extra weights gone, he stands six feet two and 175 pounds at the age of eighteen. I promised Logan I would write this book, so here it is.

The book brings to the reader many great thoughts and ideas about the game of baseball that has weathered the test of time. Over forty years of my baseball coaching experiences are in here for you to explore. I believe my aggressive coaching style helped win a lot of baseball games and helped build strong baseball programs. I've always thought the baseball field was a wonderful place to get a good hot dog and a snow cone on a hot summer night while watching players learn to compete in America's greatest game. So read and enjoy my thoughts about how to play baseball.

Coach Geigle

Chapter 1

America's Game

<u>***The Coach***</u>

The Coach

We all have our own ideas of what a good baseball coach looks like and the value they bring to a good baseball program and community. Parents want their kids to play for a coach who treats them with respect and truly cares about their development. I've always respected a coach that knows his stuff and is confident doing his job while bringing a winning spirit, a coach that demonstrates strong character that will build long-lasting relationships. I also look for a coach to be tough, knowledgeable, and able to teach solid baseball skills and fundamentals. As a spectator, I want to sit in the stands watching our team play, feeling excited that he's our coach. He does what's right at the right time, drawing from his years of experience, and communicates with honesty to the players and parents. Having said this, I realize there is no perfect coach, and I also know that there is no shortcut to a winning program. In all my years involved in baseball, I've learned that winning coaches come in many different personalities, but they all have one thing in common—they all love the game

Baseball Coaching On The Run!

Your probably looking through the book coaching baseball and thinking it's put together a little different. I'd like to explain the short titles you will find placed through out the book before each topic is discussed. For example hit the ball hard, no soft throw's, lay off the high ones along with a number of others. These short one line reminders taught us how to play the game and are ment to teach players how to talk baseball in practice and most important in the games. When the baseball season started, as a coach I only had two weeks to get the team ready for their first game. It was coaching on the run. I didn't have time in practice to stop and talk for ten or twenty minutes on how and why I wanted things a certain way. I did more talking later during the season but at the start we were in a rush. During our drills in practice I would shout out one liners and verbalize to the players how to play and what to be thinking about in differnt situation. I pushed them and held them accountable for practing the one liners I was calling out. I knew later I had done a good job when the players talked it up during a game and were using one liners learned in practice, like make sure of the first one, chest high throws, play the hop, sit down on a ground ball. I think you have the idea. I love my one liners and they helped us play better and smarter baseball.

Linfield College Wildcat Inspiration
First Day Of The Season

Date Wed, 23 Sep 1998 16:01

To: Larry Geigle

From: Craig Conway

Subject: Inspirational Quote for a Wildcat

Larry: From my wife, Katharine, an inspirational quote to me earlier this week that I feel is quite appropriate to encourage you... "It is not true that nice guys finish last. Nice guys are winners before the game even starts." .. Mr. G, you are a WINNER! You are a coach that models respect, dignity, honor, hope, disipline, fairness, integrity, and value ... that makes you a winner before the day even starts... WILDCATS always battle with a brave and mighty spirit, right? Keep up the good fight... it's worth it and if I enrolled at Linfield again and it was 1974 all over again (knowing what I know now 24 years later) I would still want to become a teacher and coach... and I firmly believe that you would make the same decision again, too! Respectfully submitted Craig...

Craig Conway, 9/23/98 8:33pm Insirational Quote for a Wildcat

---

To: Craig Conway

From: Larry Geigle

Subject: Re: Inspirational Quote for a Wildcat

It's good to have been a Wildcat ---- It's good to have known victory. I have been blessed with so many wins, it makes the defeats seem small. I do know that some seasons were better than others, but all worth the effort. I look forward everyday to the challenges of a new season. No matter when, where or how the season starts good or bad we should remember it's our desire to finish strong that counts. Yes, it's the first day of a new season and yes it looks a little out of sink. You know and I know the blue ribbion is still up for grabs and as a LINFIELD WILDCAT IT'S OUR JOB TO BRING IT HOME.

Thanks for lifting my day ---- Your a great Friend and a great teacher and a great Linfield brother.

Coach Geigle

Truck and Trailer for the Championship (Summer 1971)

Enjoy Baseballs History

of the World series

throughout Coaching Baseball

1903 Word Series Champions

Boston Americans 5 wins 3 loses

Truck and Trailer for the Championship (Summer 1971)

It is a hot summer evening in 1971, and I'm on the sidelines coaching in the championship game of one of my Cedar Hills Little League teams. I'm coaching trying to earn extra cash in the summer to work my way through college. My team is up to bat, and it's the bottom of the seventh inning and there is one out. We have Neil, our biggest and strongest base runner on third, and Harry, our speedster on second. The game is tied, and it's our last chance to win before going into extra innings. The fans are cheering. We are having a hard time hitting the ball, and our two weakest hitters are coming to the plate. We need to do something now! The only bright spot is that our two best base runners are on the bases. I decided to give the signal for our special play, "THE TRUCK AND TRAILER!" My players look at each other, and they all know what's coming. The pitcher starts his windup, and Harry, my base runner on second, takes off for third. Neil, who is on third, just stands and waits for Harry who is headed full speed his way. When Harry gets close to third, they both head for home, Harry now riding Neil's coattails. The pitcher delivers the pitch to home, and the catcher catches the ball then immediately comes out to block the plate and tag the first base runner out. Neil slams into him, knocking him to the ground; but as he goes down, he tags Neil out, but can't get back up in time to tag Harry, our second base runner, who crosses the plate a moment later. The crowd draws quiet; you couldn't hear a sound. They wait for the umpire's call. With a loud booming voice, the umpire calls the second base runner SAFE! and the crowd erupts. The opposing team can't believe what happened, and with looks of disbelief, their players look at our team as we start jumping for joy and celebrating sweet victory. Our team once again has won the Cedar Hills Little Leauge championship.

I guess you had to be there to understand the real importance of this game. My players were what you would call the leftovers, weren't supposed to be that good. I could go down the list of these guys and tell you something wonderful about each one of them and the support from their wonderful parents. I loved those types of moments, I mean, being in a situation where you had to lay it all on the line. We practiced that play over and over until we knew someday we could pull it out of our bag of surprises and it would get us through.

One of the great memories of coaching that team was Harry's swimming pool. It gets hot in the summer, and after a ball game, the whole team would head over to Harry's house. His parents would fire up the barbecue and we'd have fun talking about the game while cooling off in the large pool in their backyard. After swimming and eating hamburgers for a couple of hours, we would all head home, ready to do it all over again. What a great way to spend the summer.

<u>*Attitude, Attitude Attitude!*</u>

1904 Baseball History

World Series Cancelled

1905 World Series Champions

New York Giants 4-1

1906 world series Champions

Chicago White Sox 4-2

Attitude, Attitude, Attitude!

During my college days, I decided to play football and baseball for the Linfield Wildcats in McMinnville, Oregon. Linfield was known for its great baseball and football teams back then, and today, it still remains a respected program. The only difference between today and back when I played is the Wildcats have won three national baseball titles, three national football titles, and have the longest consecutive record for the number of winning football seasons of any college in the nation. Sixty-six years without a losing football season, that's not bad. Back when I played, I took part and witnessed this great program being born. The coaches were professional, and they did a wonderful job of showing respect and caring toward their players. At that time, my philosophy regarding playing was very simple. Do what it takes to get the job done, do it right, and do it with a smile. That's what I tried to model every day as a Wildcat. One day while I was on the field, the coach started talking with me and complimenting on how hard I worked and my great attitude in practice. He told me what a good player I was becoming and how much he appreciated my positive approach and willingness to work hard in practice. When he was done, I said thanks and told him it was great to be a Wildcat. My point in telling this story is to show how the idea of doing whatever it takes to earn my coach's respect was well worth it. His praise for a job well done always lifted me up. I always remembered that conversation with my coach and used that same approach on the baseball and football field from the day I started coaching. I lifted my players up and gave them the confidence to get the job done. They loved to hear me call out their name and simply say, "GREAT JOB!" I'm retired now, and I have a chance to look back at my effort in the different jobs I performed. Some jobs I admit were not my favorite, but just the same, my approach never changed. Back in the day and even now, my can-do approach to work and coaching formed a solid foundation for success in the years to come. During those years, I have received a lot of respect and benefitted from doing my best and working hard. If I made a mistake, I apologized and expressed how I wouldn't try to let it happen again. In my coaching, having a positive approach always paid off, and my players played better for it. There's no question I was demanding and tough during games and on the practice field, but every once in a while, I made sure the kids would see me smile so that they knew I loved them and I loved the game. To me, having a positive attitude has become one of the most important ways I found to achieve success. Not giving up, working hard, doing what's right, and building a positive atmosphere of respect on and off the field are solid lessons to being a good coach.

<u>Victory With Class!</u>

1907 World Series Champions

Chicago Cubs 4-0-1(T)

1908 World Series Champions

Chicago Cubs 4-1

Victory with Class!

We've all participated in baseball games where there have been heated discussions and confrontations between players, coaches, and umpires. After a contested game, spectators walk away talking and shaking their heads about the injustices that took place and how the other team got lucky because the umpire missed a call, causing them to lose the game. After having played and coached for years, I realized that conflicts are going to happen, errors are going to be made, and calls are going to be missed. Coaches and seasoned players understand it's part of the game and learn to walk away with class. During the game when talking to the umpires about different contested situations, coaches should communicate and explain their side of the story being respectful. We all know it's not easy being an umpire and making perfect calls every game. Even the good umpires blow it once in a while. Coaches who ride the umpire in a negative way for too long find out the hard way it reflects on their team. Umpires are human and only listen to so much negative feedback before taking appropriate action. If the spectators witness their coach getting after the umpire, they might think it's okay to start making comments that can bring about even more negativity. I've always respected the coaches in baseball who have a professional demeanor on and off the field. I believe that it carries over to the players. Remember, victory with class! Having said that, I wish I could say I was perfect, but we've all had our moments, right?

Team Leadership

In Baseball!

1909 World Series Champions

Pittsburgh Pirates 4-3

1910 World Series Champions

Philadelphia Athletics 4-1

1911 World Series Champions

Philadelphia Athletics 4-2

Team Leadership in Baseball

Every year, you can hear the start of baseball season; and once again, the sound of baseballs hitting the bat ring out as fans cheer their teams on. Every so often, a ball will fly over the fence, and the fans will go crazy with a burst of excitement as the hitter rounds the bases. Hot dogs will be cooking on the grill with popcorn and snow cones being handed out. Parents sit in stands and visit, talking about their sons and daughters. Yes, it's baseball season once again, and the sun is out, bringing warmth to the ballpark. As we listen to the sounds of baseball teams cheering and coaches trying to push their players to be their very best, we realize it is some of the best moments we will remember with our kids. Every new year brings a new group of players who are asked to pass on the torch for a winning season. They are also asked to practice toughness, perfection, brotherhood, and respect for each other. Those who are returning players are given the responsibility of setting the tone for the new players. At the end of the first practice, players will come together and talk about what's expected and the effort needed to achieve success. As a coach, I believe the birth of leadership along with becoming a stronger person takes place by being part of a baseball team. It's a time for players to walk their talk and set the right example in handling tough situations on the baseball field. They've been taught to play with respect for each other, coaches, and umpires while learning America's greatest game. Parents look to coaches to watch over the team, making sure baseball is a positive experience for players, parents, and the community. Coaches give responsibility to young people, which can be very powerful and a great opportunity for them to grow. This is shown with each passing week as teams rise up and show outstanding performances that reach new levels of success and confidence. Week after week, the players work hard, getting ready to compete in the next game. Then on a hot summer night, players set the tone to compete to win and not give up. When the team is victorious, the coaches teach players to be humble and also respectful in defeat while holding their heads up and showing good sportsmanship.

Chapter 2

Baseball Secrets

PRACTICE AND REPETITION!

1912 World Series Champions

Boston Red Sox 4-3

1913 World Series Champions

Philadelphia Athletics 4-1

1914 World Series Champions

Boston Braves 4-0

1915 World Series Champions

Boston Red Sox 4-1

Practice and Repetition

Practice and repetition are two of the true secrets to becoming truly good at your craft. Through many hours of practice, you become aware and sensitive to the small important details that set you apart from others. You learn to feel, smell, touch, hear, and see the secrets to becoming better. During hundreds of hours of practice and repetition, you will experience many victories and some defeats. Celebrate the victories and hold them close; they will give you the confidence to move forward. Learn from the defeats, and remember what you learned. Don't dwell on the losses; let it pass and don't look back. Continue your journey. Remember, defeats are part of the process to greatness. At times, you might need to step back and take a break, reflecting on where you've been and where you're headed. Even then during your break, without knowing it, you will still be growing and processing the secrets you have learned. The truly good players (coaches) come from seasoned veterans who over the years have acquired wisdom and skill through practice, repetition, and most of all, time.

____

____

____

____

____

Practice Tempo
And
Accountability!

1916 World Series Champions

Boston Red Sox 4-1

1917 World Series Champions

Chicago White Sox 4-2

1918 World Series Champions

Boston Red Sox 4-2

Practice Tempo and Accountability

Practice and repetition are lost without accountability and tempo. Your individual players as well as the team as a whole improvement depend on what type of atmosphere you develop in practice. Baseball is a sport played in a time-sensitive and competitive environment. Going through practice at a slow noncompetitive pace and not insisting that your players perform is the road toward average at best. Performing at an upbeat practice tempo sets the stage for your players to be in better physical shape, catch more baseballs, hit better, make more plays, and win more games. The list goes on and on. If your team isn't working hard in practice, then it's your job as a coach to light a fire under their camera (butt) and give them a reason to try harder. It's more important that the players respect coaches first and like them second. Practice tempo is one of the secrets to success on the baseball field. Lazy talent is inconsistent and will lead to average play and a lack of success under pressure.

<u>Play As Much Baseball</u>

<u>As You Can!</u>

1919 World Series Champions

Cincinnati Reds 5-3

1920 World Series Champions

Cleveland Indians 5-2

1921 World Series Champions

New York Giants 5-3

Play as Much Baseball as You Can!

As a coach, I always thought it was important for young players to play as much baseball as they could. During the summer of 1993, I was an assistant coach for Sunset High School's American Legion baseball program in Beaverton, Oregon. We were excited to hit the road and travel throughout the state of Oregon playing doubleheaders almost every day. Our kids had a reputation of being good ballplayers, and we live up to that reputation of being tough to beat. Most of our games were against other legion teams in Oregon, like Eugene, Roseburg, Grants Pass, Medford, Salem, and the Portland area. We also played some pretty good semipro teams along our journey. That summer, the sun beat down on our players every day, and they quickly acquired dark tans and a leather toughness that was sometimes hard to believe. We usually started playing around two o'clock in the afternoon and wouldn't be done with the second game until ten that night. It was always hot with the temperature hitting the nineties to a hundred degrees. Even though our players just finished playing a doubleheader, they would always want to play more baseball by catching some fly balls in the outfield and taking some grounders in the infield. We did this as we enjoyed the beautiful summer nights relaxing under the field lights. You just couldn't wear these guys out. Other teams would be headed home, but our players were still wanting to play baseball. When we were done, it was back to the hotel and a good night's sleep, just to do it all over again the next night. This group of players was completely absorbed in baseball every day. We asked them to play against the best teams in Oregon, and they found themselves in hundreds of defensive and offensive situations. As a result, they grew to be very comfortable on the field and away from home traveling on the road. They could all play many different positions, and our pitchers were outstanding. When the players took infield before a game, they looked like a fine-tuned machine making strong throws and turning double plays like they were nothing. It didn't surprise me the following year when they went on to claim the 1994 Oregon High School 5A state baseball title. I'll never forget that summer of 1993 and how much fun we had and how we loved the game. This group of players dedicated themselves to working hard and playing hundreds of games growing up. They were a great group of guys that enjoyed each other's company and always gave it up for the team. My point is very simple—the more you play the game, the better player you will become. The 1994 high school champions at Sunset High School in Beaverton, Oregon, truly earned their title.

<u>Hit Before Every Game!</u>

1922 World Series Champions

New York Giants 4-0

1923 World Series Champions

New York Yankees 4-2

1924 World Series Champions

Washington Senators 4-3

1925 World Series Champions

Pittsburgh Pirates 4-3

Hit Before Every Game!

Hitting and bunting practice before a baseball game has always been an important part of players' success in games. Taking cuts at the baseballs helps create momentum mentally and physically to hit at a high level in the upcoming game. Throwing batting practice by lobbing the ball across the plate is not my idea of a good warm-up. I threw batting practice hard and came away dripping wet with sweat. I always carried a towel and clean T-shirt with me to change into when I was done throwing. It's a lot of work, but I felt my players hit better against good pitching. I also thought they respected my effort to get them ready to hit. After we hit, we jumped right into one bunt drill. The outfielders would form a line down an imaginary first baseline and the infielders down an imaginary third baseline. Alternating lines one at a time, they would step up to an imaginary plate and would get one pitch to lay it down correctly then go to the end of their line. Each perfect bunt would be worth a point. The first team to ten points won. My assistant coach threw the bunting practice three-fourth speed. The team that won one bunt didn't have to clean up the gear after the upcoming game. When we were done, I thought we were ready to play ball. I always felt my players were better hitters because of my little bag of hitting drills. Later in the book, I'll explain some of my hitting thoughts and secrets. You will read about my success in hitting tennis balls and teaching the players how to hit the ball hard. You will also read about my bunting drills and holding players accountable for good bunts using team competition.

Watching Other Teams Warm Up!

1926 World Series Champion

St Louis Cardinals 4-3

1927 World Series Champios

New Yook Yankees 4-0

1928 Worls Series Champions

New York Yankees 40

1929 World Series Champions

Philadelphia Athletics 4-1

Watching Other Teams' Warm-Up

It's always good to watch the other teams' warm-ups before a game to see which of their players have strong arms and how well they field the baseball. It's also good to watch the catcher and determine his ability and accuracy to throw runners out. Lazy and slow infield and outfield warm-ups send a message to me as a coach. I will steal more bunt more and be more aggressive if I think the opposing team is daydreaming. I will hold them accountable for not being prepared and put pressure on their defense to make plays and field the ball. Having said that, some teams and some players can surprise you even though they look one way then completely surprise you with their ability in a game. I always want to know the opposing team's roster and win-loss record before we play. I want to know who on their team can make the big plays.

Play With Character And Confidence!

1930 World Series Champions

Philadelphia Athletics 4-2

1931 World Series Champions

St Louis Cardinals 4-3

1932 World Series Champios

New York Yankees 40

1933 World Series Champions

New York Giants 4-1

Play with Character and Confidence

Baseball is not a sport for the weak. It demands that you give it your full attention with hundreds of hours hitting, catching, and throwing the baseball. To become a great player, you must play with strong character and good sportsmanship. The real fans of baseball realize that standing at the plate with a ninety-three-mile-an-hour fastball coming at your head takes courage and skill to avoid getting hit and then hitting the next pitch out of the park. We watch these athletes playing doubleheaders every day in hundred-degree heat with the sun bearing down on them for hours during a game. Then if you're not playing a game, you're at practice fine-tuning your skills. You can recognize these real players by their dedication, dark tans, confidence, along with a keen developed sense of humor from hours, days, weeks, and years of playing the game. The great players over time understand there's no shortcut to true victory. They always, and I mean always, have their teammates back.

<u>*Lift Your Team Mates Up*</u>
<u>*Don't Bring Them Down!*</u>

1934 World Series Champions

St. Louis Cardinals 4-3

1935 World Series Champions

Detroit Tigersm 4-2

1936 World Series Champions

New York Yankees 4-2

Lift Your Teammates Up, Don't Bring Them Down!

There's no question why lifting players up after they've made a mistake is the right thing to do. You always want your players to play with confidence and poise. Coaches or teammates being negative is no way to build a successful baseball program. Everyone should realize no one wants to do poorly. I've witnessed coaches destroy players' confidence by treating them bad. The end result is the player makes even more mistakes and develops negative feelings toward the coach and the program. This type of coaching produces a nonproductive atmosphere and brings the team down. To help players play their best baseball, remember to lift them up. Help everyone work hard and believe in themselves. I always thought the sound of my voice giving praise as a coach could ignite players and lift them to a new confidence in themselves. When a player makes a great play, be excited, compliment him, and be happy for their success. When a mistake occurs, acknowledge what has happened, learn from it, and continue to stay focused while getting better and having fun playing. Having said that, as a coach, I have pushed my teams at times and let them know they need to work harder. You might say I lit a fire under their butts. *Notice I said "teams." I never try to single out a player in front of the rest of the team. If I have something to discuss with a player, I will find the right time and place to talk with him.* I always wanted as a coach to let my players know I appreciated their efforts. Remember, lift up your teammate and lift up your team; it is the right thing to do.

Cheer A Great Play!

1937 World Series Champions

New York Yankees 4-1

1938 World Series Champions

New York Yankees 4-0

1939 World Series Champions

New york Yankees 40

1940 World Seriers Champion

Cincinnati Reds 4-3

Cheer a Great Play!

I'm sure you've witnessed a baseball player hit one out of the park. Everyone jumps out of their seat and throws their arms up to go crazy for just a few minutes. Teammates start jumping around congratulating each other as they watch their teammate who hit a home run round the bases and cross the home plate to bring the team one play closer to winning the game. Teammates understand that cheering a great play or a great hit is why we show up at the ballpark. It's fun, and great plays don't happen very often; but when it does, it's time to party and cheer for your team as well as the great game of baseball. It's a special moment for everyone. Remember, whether it's a great catch or home run, be ready to cheer your team on and create a special moment.

Don't Hang Your Head!

1941 World Series Champions

New York Yankees 4-1

1942 World Series Champions

St. Louis Cardinals 4-1

1943 World Series Champions

New York Yankees 4-1

1944 World Series Champions

St. Louis Cardinals 4-2

Don't Hang Your Head!

Not hanging your head in a baseball game after you have made an error is easier said than done. If everyone plays the game perfectly, no one would win. Making mistakes is part of playing baseball that everyone eventually must deal with. Hanging your head will bring your team down very quickly. The one person that can stop this from happening is the player that made the mistake. He's the guy who needs to stay fired up and come back with a great play and send a strong message that the game isn't over. Great teams continue to believe in each other in adverse situations and know they will find a way to even up the score. Good teams and great players support each other, staying strong, making sure they have each other's back. The great teams believe they will eventually win.

Answer A Bad Play
With A Great Play Or Hit!

1945 World Series Champions

Detroit Tigers 4-3

1946 World Series Champions

St Louis Cardinals 4-3

1947 World Series Champuions

New York Yankees 4-3

1948 World Series Champion

Cleveland Indians 4-2

Answer a Bad Play with a Great Play or Hit!

Answering a bad play with a good play is the true mark of a champion in any sport. Sitting in the bleachers, I always look for the players who won't get down on themselves when they have just made a bad play. You can watch and observe their determination to come back with great effort to even things up. This type of competitor is hard to beat and exciting to watch and cheer for. Anyone who plays baseball knows that errors are going to happen. How the player deals with the situation is important to his own mindset in the field as well as up the plate and to the rest of the team. Coming back with a good play can lift your team up and ignite the fans watching. Remember, in baseball, there are many different variables taking place, and your performance will be remembered and evaluated over time by hundreds of plays, not by one or two mistakes. To help eliminate making bad plays, make sure you're ready and awake and in the game. Know the situation, and finally, practice, practice, practice.

Chapter 3

Pitching

Throw Strikes

No Wild Pitches

No Walks!

1949 World Series Champions

New York Yankees 4-1

1950 World Series Champion

New York Yankees 4-0

1951 World Series Champions

New York Yankees 4-2

1952 World Series Champions

New York Yankees 4-3

Throw Strikes! No Wild Pitches! No Walks!

Here's some good advice for coaches as well as players. If you want to win baseball games, then remember this! Throw good pitches and be able to hit the different locations on the plate. To do this well, spend time in practice charting your pitches and keeping track of your accuracy and the locations. Doing this, you will realize your strongest pitching tendency for accuracy. Spend time during games watching the other team's hitters and their stance at the plate; try to watch their hitting weaknesses and where they've hit the ball. Good baseball teams keep an updated history of opponents and their hitting ability; study this information. Also, don't forget who bunts the ball well in your opponent's lineup. There's no question keeping this information is a lot of work, but in the end, it may help your team win some games. When you are out on the mound throwing pitches in a game, here's a good rule to remember: throw the ball inside and high to jam a batter so he can't get the bat around or throw it low and away to make him reach for the ball while taking his power away. Remember, ball games are lost because pitchers can't throw the ball accurately or where it needs to hit the strike zone. They end up walking batters or throwing a wild pitch and moving base runners up on the bases. There's also the other side of the coin where pitchers are being too fine or trying too hard to place the ball for location and end up getting behind in the count and putting batters on base. A simple rule is no more than two walks in a game and no wild pitches. These expectations are high, I know, but it helps send the message to pitchers that part of winning is not walking batters, not throwing wild pitches, and not helping base runners move up on the bases. As a pitcher, you should always work hard to stay ahead on the count and keep base runners off the bases. Base runners add pressure to pitching and can take away from the pitchers' effectiveness to throw strikes.

<u>Pitcher's Quick Release</u>

<u>On The Wind up!</u>

1953 World Series Champions

New York Yankees 4-2

1954 World Series Champions

New York Giants 4-0

1955 World Series Champions

Brooklyn Dodgers 4-3

Pitcher's Quick Release on the Windup!

A good windup or stretch from the pitcher's mound will go a long way to help win ball games. Pitchers with a quick release help hold base runners on and keep them from getting good jumps stealing bases. The other advantage with a pitcher's quick release is the ball arrives at the plate sooner and gives the catcher a better chance of throwing a base runner out. It also helps when the opposing team is trying to bunt the ball with a man on base. The ball once again arrives at plate sooner and makes it easier for the catcher to catch the ball, field a bunt, or tag a base runner coming home. When the opposing team studies a pitcher and realizes his quick release, it makes them think twice about stealing or bunting the ball. It's just the opposite; if they see a slow release, then without a doubt, they will use it to their advantage.

<u>Stretch With A Man On Base!</u>

1956 World Series Champions

New York Yankees 4-3

1957 World Series Canceled

1958 World Series Canceled

1959 World Series Champions

Los Angeles Dodgers 4-2

The Stretch with a Man on Base!

With a man on base, a pitcher should always stretch. The only exception is when there is a man on third base and the game is not close. In that situation, a pitcher should use his windup. When the game is close, the pitcher should use the stretch to keep the runner close to third in case they try to bunt or steal home. Pitchers should always stretch with a base runner on first or second base, no exceptions! The purpose of the stretch is to help achieve a much quicker release to the plate than you get from a windup. You're trying to get the ball to the catcher sooner and keep base runners from stealing. When using the stretch, vary your timing on the rubber before throwing the pitch, also vary your looks at the base runner to hold them on. For example, one look, then two looks, then two looks, and back to one look; mix it up, keep the base runner guessing. Try not to get into a rhythm where your delivery to the plate is the same every pitch. When you do this, it helps to hold the runner; and then when you do use your pickoff move, it might catch the base runner leading too far off the base or leaning. When pitching from the stretch, to be effective, your pickoff move to a base must be quick and have a purpose. You should know ahead of time who might steal a base. I always coach my players to look for the aggressive base runners who are fast and can steal. The great pickoff moves are when no one expects it coming. Be sure your defensive player is ready to catch the ball to make the tag. If you see the base runner let down for a moment and start napping, that's the moment you can pick them off.

Chapter 4

Base Running

When Running The Bases Touch All The bags!

1960 World Series Champions

Pittsburgh Pirates 4-3

1961 World Series Champions

New York Yankees 4-1

1962 World Series Champions

New York Yankees 4-3

1963 World Series Champions

Los Angeles Dodgers 4-0

When Running the Bases, Touch All the Bags

This is a very short, but very important reminder to touch all the bases when running. When running and approaching a base on a single or long hit, use the inside corner of the base to push off as you make your turn. When on a base and you know you can't leave until the ball is caught, put your feet in a position with your foot on the base to help you push off. Be in a sprinter stance when the ball gets caught then push off. Be smart; try not to get caught in a rundown or hotbox. Listen to your base coach whether to go or not, and always tag up on a fly ball.

When On Base

Get A Good Lead!

1964 World Series Champions

St. Louis Cardinals 4-3

1965 World Series Champions

Los Angeles Dodgers 4-3

1966 World Series Champions

Baltimore Orioles 4-0

1967 Worls Series Champions

St. Louis Cardinals 4-3

When on Base, Get a Good Lead

When you're on base, it's important that you know where the baseball is at all times. I teach pitchers to study base runners to see if they're paying attention when they're on base. Every once in a while, the base runner will drop his eyes or look somewhere else while taking a lead; that's when you pick him. So if you're a base runner, you must keep your eyes and head in the game at all times. Make sure you listen to the base coach and watch his hands when you slide or make a turn when you're running. The secret is to take advantage of what's given to you; for example, a wild pitch or a catcher's bad throw back to the pitcher. Maybe the catcher will try to throw the ball behind you after the pitch if you lead off too far, and he throws down to first making a wild throw into right field. After you dive back to the base, bounce up, be ready to advance to second base if possible. Always be ready to tag up on fly balls to the outfield and be ready to go. Know when to slide into a base. Know how to hook slide, headfirst slide, or dive back to the base. Practice and be ready to use these slides in a ball game. Know the situation when you're on base. If the other team is slow or lazy getting the ball back to the infield, steal a base; make them pay. If the pitcher has a slow turn to throw to first, take advantage of it, take a bigger lead. Take an extra step when you lead off trying to make the pitcher look at you and even better make him nervous. Some pitchers have trouble delivering the pitch with an aggressive base runner acting like he's going to steal the base. I know I jumped around a lot, but all these points are important to win ball games. The younger the players, the more pressure you put on their defense. That might sound aggressive, but that's baseball.

When On Base

Always Be Ready

For A Wild Pitch!

1968 World Series Champions

Detroit Tigers 4-3

1969 World Series Champions

New York Mets 4-1

1970 World Series Champions

Baltimore Orioles 4-1

1971 World Series Champions

Pittsburgh Pirates 4-3

When on Base, Always Be Ready for a Wild Pitch!

I can't tell you how many times I've sat in the bleachers watching missed opportunities by base runners to steal a base on a wild pitch. I always coach my players that every pitch is a potentially wild pitch and to be ready to steal a base. Remember, when you take your lead and the pitch is headed toward the plate, be aggressive and get off the bag. If the pitcher has a slow pickoff move or a slow delivery, take one or two extra strides with the idea the catcher might miss the pitch. If the catcher catches the pitch, always return to the base quickly knowing he might throw behind you to the base. I always coach a right-hand dive back to the base if the pitcher makes a move and tries to pick a runner or the catcher tries to throw back door down to the base. Timing in leading off is important. Extending the lead at the right moment when the catcher misses the pitch gives the base runner a great jump stealing a base and maybe even home to score a run.

When On Base
Always Watch The Ball!

1972 World Series Champions

Oakland Athletics 4-3

1973 World Series Champions

Oakland Athletics 4-3

1974 World Series Champions

Oakland Athletics 4-1

1975 World Series Champions

Cincinnati Reds 4-3

When on Base Always Watch the Ball

When base running, players need to be alert and be in the game at all times. Before they step off the bag, they need to find the baseball and know what's happening on the field. When at bat and running down to first base on a bunt, infield ground ball, or strike three dropped pitch by the catcher, they should run through first base and quickly get under control in case a defensive player makes a wild throw. Anytime you're on base, find the baseball, listen to your base coach when advancing to the next base for his signal to get down (slide), or take another base. As a base runner, be looking for an opportunity to surprise the other team and steal another base when they're not paying attention. Base running is an art, and the great base runners are very aware of what's going on and waiting to take advantage of the other team's mistakes.

Bobbling The Ball In The Outfield!

1976 World Series Champions

Cincinnati Reds 4-0

1977 World Series Champions

New York Yankees 4-2

1978 World Series Champions

New York Yankees 4-2

1979 World Series Champions

Pittsbrugh Pirates 4-3

Bobbling the Ball in the Outfield!

During a game, if an outfielder tries to field hard-hit ground ball and bobbles it, the base runner who is running the bases should take a good turn and head to next base unless the base coach tells him to hold up. I found that fielders who bobble the ball will hurry to get control of the baseball, pick it up, and make a hurried throw to the base, missing the bag, thus giving the base runner a free base.

Chapter 5

Hitting

Knowing Your Strike Zone!

1980 World Series Champions

Philadelphia Phillies 4-2

1981 World Series Champions

Los Angeles Dodgers 4-2

1982 World Series Champions

St. Louis Cardinals 4-3

1983 World Series Champions

Baltimore Orioles 4-1

Knowing Your Strike Zone!

During the summer while I was attending college, I worked as a baseball instructor for Parks and Recreation in Beaverton, Oregon. My job from 8:00 a.m. to 10:00 a.m. was to teach the little guys how to play baseball. Back then, we didn't have hitting tees, so we pitched to the kids up close and threw the ball to their strike zone. It wasn't easy for young kids to hit the ball so you waited for the big hits, but by the end of the summer, they were on their way and making contact with the ball and excited about swinging the bat. During the rest of the day from 10:00 a.m. to 4:00 p.m., I would coach two different older age groups, each having their own team. After just a few practices with the older players, I thought for their age they weren't being aggressive enough at the plate. They were too picky, and they wanted to see the perfect pitch before swinging. I began to push the players to hit anything close to the plate. I realized the pitching in the games wouldn't be perfect, and we needed to hit the ball to win some games. I wanted to see more contact with the ball and more players on the bases, making other teams play good defense to beat us. After my long-winded speeches, a short time later, players started to demonstrate a more aggressive attitude at the plate and hit the ball better and harder. Even my weak hitters were hitting the ball and gaining a lot of confidence. I also set up hitting stations in practice for hitting the ball live and bunting. I used an old tennis ball machine to fire hundreds of tennis balls at the player's strike zone. The players started swinging the bat more and getting hundreds of cuts while working on watching the ball and gaining confidence at the plate. I tried to push the players to hit the ball hard every day. You could see they weren't afraid of being hit by the tennis balls, so they stood relaxed at the plate hitting rockets and watching the tennis balls fly over the fence. This newfound confidence carried over to hitting a real baseball in the games. The players were becoming comfortable and disciplined hitters with swagger and power. Sometimes I thought the sound of my voice ignited their hitting ability; I knew they loved to hear me yelling at them to hit the ball hard and saying "great job!" The older players became very successful for the next two years, winning league championships at two different age levels.

Knowing your strike zone comes from many hours standing at the plate watching hundreds and even thousands of pitched baseballs fly by and picking which ones to hit. There's no shortcut to hitting a baseball or perfecting a great swing. For most players, it's seeing the pitch and recognizing its location. The real seasoned hitters stand at the plate with confidence and work hard at not swinging at bad pitches. They're trying to figure out when the pitcher is going to throw a hitting pitch and being ready to jump on it. Most pitchers will try to take away a hitter's power by throwing the baseball inside and high. They do this to jam your ability to swing the bat. Good hitters will see the inside pitch coming, turn on it early, and hit the ball out in front of the plate, sending it down the third baseline and into left field. Pitchers will also try taking hitter's power away by throwing the ball on the outside of the plate low and away to make the hitter reach for the ball and once again taking their power away. In this case, a seasoned hitter will wait on the ball and hit it late, sending it down the first base side of the field and to right field. Most young pitchers will try to develop at least three great pitches to strike out hitters. One might be the fast ball. In this case, the pitcher tries to blow the baseball by the hitter who swings late and can't get his bat around quick enough to hit the ball. Then there is the curve ball. The pitcher throws the baseball with a high-velocity spin that makes the ball look like it's coming right at you and, to the batter's surprise, curves back in over the plate at the last moment, keeping the batter completely off balance. One more pitch in a pitcher's bag of tricks might be the changeup. This pitch is delivered by pitchers who throw a great fast ball, and it looks like they're going to throw another fast ball across the plate and, to the batter's surprise, the ball comes in like a slow-pitch softball, making the batter lunge, swinging too early. Other pitches might include the screwball, the knuckleball, and the drop ball. All these pitches are good ideas at the right time and effective if the pitcher can hit the strike zone and keep the batter off balance.

Hitting The Ball Hard!

1984 World Series Champions

Detroit Tigers 4-1

1985 World Series Champions

Kansas City Royals 4-3

1986 World Series Champions

New York Mets 4-3

1987 World Series Champions

Minnesota Twins 4-3

Hitting The Ball Hard!

Hitting the baseball hard is important for young players to remember. If I'm sitting up in the bleachers watching a baseball game you can bet I'll be looking for players to hit the ball hard. The younger the player the more I encourage it. Many younger players look like the bats swinging them not them swinging the bat. Young players should look for a bat that is right for their size and strength so they swing with control. We all as young hitters wanted to use a bigger bat. Remembering back to when I was a young player I would try to make contact with a big bat because I thought the ball would travel a longer distance. The trouble was, the bat was so heavy I couldn't control it or get it around quick enough to hit the ball. The heavy bat produced an upward slow looking swing with very little bat speed. If you use a bat thats the right size it will help you meet the ball and help you generate more power and your swing will look better and feel right.

Here is a little story that illustrates me teaching my daughter how to hit the ball hard and having fun at it. One afternoon many years ago when I was a very young coach. My oldest daughter and I went out on the front lawn with one of those big over sized plastic bats you buy at K Mart which comes with a plastic wiffel ball. Once we were out on the grass I handed her the bat and told her to get in her hitting stance. I'm sure she wondered what I was doing. I explained to my daughter that I wanted her to swing the bat and take her best shot at hitting me on the butt while I was bent over. She just looked at me with a smile and said really! I then bent over and told her to swing the bat hard. She couldn't believe what I wanted her to do but, she had a smile on her face and she was getting a free shot at smacking her dad in the butt with big red plastic bat. Her first swing like most young players was soft and barley made a statement. I turned and expressed to her that she was a light weight and she swung the bat like an old rusty gate. She got kind of a funny look on her as to say ok lets try it again. Thats all it took, the next time she swung it was hard and hit me square in the butt. The plastic bat rang out with a loud smacking sound that turn the neighbors head accross the street. My daughter laughed' but you could see she was impressed with the power of her swing and the sound of the bat hitting dads butt. After a few more powerful swings my butt was feeling it, so I pulled out a tennis ball stood back and threw her a few pitches. When she hit the first ball her swing was so powerful and aggressive, it went sailing over the house accross the street. She stood their with a giant smile and wanted to hit agian. The next pitch when hit came whistling past my head, I turned and watched as it sailed down to the end of our street. Again I saw the smile, I had her now, she continued to hit and love every minute of it. She was swinging the bat with great power. I had found a way to teach young hitters and my daughter how to hit the ball hard. From that time I never had to tell her to swing the bat hard again. She always loved to hear the crack of the ball meeting the bat! Through out my years of coaching if I had players who weren't swinging the bat hard I would stop by K Mart buy one of those big red plastic bats and take it to practice. I would tell one of the players to take a stance next to the dug out and swing the bat hard and hit the side of the building. It was always the same story, when he took his first swing it lacked power. I would then challenge him to swing the bat hard and feel the power behind his swing, in most cases the rest of the team would stop what they were doing and watch. The next swing the player took was strong and powerful as the plastic bat smacked the dug out. The hitters eyes open wide as a light bulb went on in his head. You could see for the first time he felt the power of a bat in his hands. The sound of the bat landing against the building had made statement to him, to swing the bat hard. You could also hear my encouragement telling the player great job! The player stood their for a moment with a smile on his face, letting everyone know this is great fun. The rest of the team came over to get in line. They too wanted to feel and hear the power of their swing against the side of the dug out. After everyone had a chance to swing the bat now called **BIG RED** you could see the poor bat was now beat to death but, all the players were starting to swing the bat with more power. Every once in while I'll stop by K Mart and buy another **BIG RED**, take it to practice and let the players smack the side of that dug out. By the way that year we set a new record for home runs. We went from 7 home runs in a season to 48 home runs over the fence in our twenty one game schedule. We were rated second in the state and set a new record for our baseball program.

Swinging the Bat

Swinging the Bat

A batter's stance varies with different hitters when they are at the plate. In most cases, if they are making contact with the ball, their swings may start out looking different, but they all end up looking the same when the bat meets the baseball. It's a good idea at a young age to focus on the fundamentals to help young hitters become great hitters as they get older. Here's what I look for in a hitter's stance. The feet are shoulder-width apart and balanced; knees are slightly bent, and the toes are pigeon-toed in. Grip the bat one inch from the bottom with your hands together, upper hand palm up and your lower hand palm down. Your middle knuckles should line up while you hold the bat away from your body with the front elbow down and your back elbow up and angled toward the ground. The bat barrel should lie back at a forty-five-degree slant while your hands are back and your shoulder is in line with your hip and back knee. While waiting for the pitch, the bat should have a small amount of waggle movement created by the arms and hands. The reason for this is simple—it's easier to swing the bat if the bat is already in motion. The motion helps you get ready to generate bat speed. Your head should be in the middle of your body with the chin on your front shoulder looking and waiting for the pitch. Your head should be still and not move around, remaining in the middle of your body during the entire swing. When swinging the bat, throw your hands toward the ball, and the bat follows. Keep your back elbow tight to your body the entire swing. The tighter the elbow, the more power you will generate. When swinging, you should be hitting against a firm front leg to keep your weight on your back leg and body behind the ball. This helps to create the correct axis for your body to turn on. Just before swinging, cock and load your body by drawing the bat back sharply a few inches. When the pitch is coming, take a soft stride with your front foot, pointing your toes back toward the pitcher. When swinging the bat, your body should turn to open up your hips to generate maximum power. You should be pivoting on your back toe with your heel up. Swing through the ball and finish up with a full swing.

When coaching young kids, I didn't want them to swing up at the ball, so I would tell them to swing the bat over the shoulder to keep their bat up. I felt this helped with meeting the ball on a level plane. Sometimes I felt their bat was just too heavy at a young age. I also wanted to see them hit line drives. It made sense that if the bat traveled toward the pitched baseball at a reduced angle, the chance of hitting the ball was much greater.

Over the years, I have come to realize that there are two types of hitters. The first is the offensive hitter. This hitter stands at the plate and starts to swing the bat at every pitch baseball. After seeing the pitch on its way, if they don't like what they see, they will break down and wait for another pitch. Offensive hitters are aggressive and have a mindset to hit every pitched ball until they can't. The second type of hitter is a defensive hitter. This hitter stands at the plate and watches the pitch as it comes to the plate. He makes his decision to swing after watching the pitch longer than the offensive hitter; he's not trying to hit every pitch. The defensive hitter is looking for the pitch he knows he can hit. At the young age group I was coaching, I always felt I wanted my players to be offensive hitters; and as they grew older, they could learn to wait for their pitch. At their age, I felt it was important to go after the ball and hit hundreds of pitches to become comfortable.

Points to Remember
Hitting the Ball

Points to Remember Hitting the Ball

1. Feet shoulder-width apart, legs slightly bent, stance balanced and relaxed.
2. Toes are pigeon-toed in.
3. Grip the bat one inch from the bottom with the upper hand palm up and lower hand palm down. Hands are together with the middle knuckles lined up.
4. Hold the bat away from your body with your front elbow angled down and your back elbow raised and angled down slightly. The bat should lie back at a forty-five-degree angle.
5. Your back shoulder should be lined up with your back knee.
6. While waiting for the pitch, your bat should have a small amount of (waggle) movement. You should be relaxed with your chin on your front shoulder.
7. Your head should be in the middle of your body and still during the entire swing.
8. Just before you swing, you cock and load your bat back a few inches. Seeing the pitch, you take a soft stride with your front foot toward the pitcher, landing with a firm front leg, then throwing your hands toward the ball with your bat following with a full swing through the ball.
9. During the swing, pivot on your back foot with your heel up. Remember to rotate and open up your hips. Keep your back elbow tight to your body for more power.
10. Swing throw the ball and finish with your chin resting on your back shoulder. Hit the ball hard!

Lay Off The High Ones!

1988 World Series Champions

Los Angeles Dodgers 4-1

1989 World Series Champions

Oakland Athletics 4-0

1990 World Series Champions

Cincinnati Reds 4-0

1991 World Series Champions

Minnesota Twins 4-3

Lay Off the High Ones

Laying off the high ones is easier said than done. I don't know what it is about high pitches, but some hitters just can't leave the high ones alone. When pitchers know the hitter's weakness for the high pitch, they'll give them what they want all night long. Unless the hitter has the ability to raise his shoulder level up to contact the ball squarely, the ball is either going to be fouled off or driven into the ground for the easy out. Hitters should stay away from the high pitch and wait for the ball to be thrown in the strike zone. When the ball is contacted on an even plane, it has a much better chance of being driven through the infield to the outfield for a base hit. Being a disciplined hitter takes many hours, days, and years to hit the baseball in different areas of the plate.

Lay The First Bunt Down!

1992 World Series Champions

Toronto Blue Jays 4-2

1993 Worls Series Champions

Toronto Blue Jays 4-2

1994 World Series Champions

Cancelled

1995 Worls Series Champions

Atlanta Braves 4-2

Lay the First Bunt Down

During my coaching career, I've found that using the bunt in a baseball game at the right time can give your team a real advantage and morale boost. When the team is in a real defensive battle and you need to generate some runs, the bunt can help. In a close game, try this—start out by getting a base runner on first with a walk, then steal second, and last, bunt your base runner down to third. Now you have created a great opportunity to score with a man on third with less than two outs while putting pressure on the other team not to make any defensive mistakes. Coaches over the years have called this type of baseball small ball. Good coaches know how to play small, and they're good at it. Good teams practice bunting every day, trying to make sure they are ready to lay the first pitch down. Coaches and players realize when you can't bunt the ball at the right moment, you're giving up your opportunity to surprise the opposing team. Good bunters not only can lay the first pitch down, but they also bunt the ball consistently in good locations. To help your bunting, try this drill—split your team up into two groups and have them compete against each other. Line up one group on the first baseline and the other group on the third baseline. Put baseball helmets out on the infield where you want the baseballs to be bunted. Alternate one player at a time from each group to step up to home plate and receive one pitch to try and bunt the ball into the helmets. If the bunt goes in a helmet, it is a point. The first team to put ten bunts in the helmets wins; the losing team puts the equipment away. Players loved to compete, and this drill can improve our ability to bunt the first pitch to consistent locations. Teams that lay their two bunts down at the end of their turn hitting in practice are average bunters at best. Good bunting teams spend the extra time getting a real feel for bunting and actually learn to put the ball where they want. Stance for bunting the ball looks like this—they start with their normal hitting stance, trying not to give the bunt away. They wait till the end of the pitcher's windup then pivot around on their front and back toes facing the pitcher. The bunter's knees are slightly bent, and he's in a crouched position. The arms are flexed with the bat out in front and eye level. The hands are split with the right hand on the balance point of the bat and your left hand toward the bottom of the handle. The bat rests on the trigger finger of your right hand and the back of your thumb. The left hand grips the bottom of the handle and helps control the bat's up-and-down movement. When the ball meets the bat, you should deaden the ball by pulling back or catching the ball with the bat and feeling the impact. To deaden the ball takes time and practice. Remember, the bat should be eye level and the barrel out over the plate. If the pitch is low, your body should sink with pitch or rise up if the pitch is high. The angle of the bat determines which direction the bunted ball will travel. Practicing the bunt is a true art, and when you've got the technique down and your bunts are consistent, it's a lot of fun. The biggest mistake I see when watching bunters would be reaching for the ball and not keeping the bat at eye level. When they do this, the number of adjustments and angles increase, and their consistency goes way down. Remember, the bat should be eye level and your head should be slightly left of the barrel. Good Luck at bunting!

The First Pitch Determines

What The Next Pitch Will Be!

1996 World Series Champions

New York Yankees 4-2

1997 World Series Champions

Florida Marlins 4-3

1998 World Series Champions

New York Yankees 4-0

1999 World Series Champions

New York Yankees 4-0

The First Pitch Determines What's the Next Pitch

Determining what the next pitch will be is one way of staying ahead of the pitcher and getting a hit or getting on base. Pitchers would like to strike you out with as few pitches as possible. If you've been hitting the baseball consistently, then the pitcher will respect your ability and use his different pitches to try to hit the corners of the plate inside and high or low and away. He will try to mix up the type of pitches to keep you off balance and guessing what's coming next. I see a lot of pitchers lead off with a fastball for a strike to get ahead in the count. Be ready for this and hit the first pitch if it's in the strike zone. If he missed and the count is 1 and 0, then you're ahead and the pitcher will fight back to get on top as they say in baseball. Expect him to throw a fastball inside high if you're crowding the plate and low and away if you're back from the plate. Remember, you're up on the count, and you can be a little more careful picking your pitch to hit. If the pitcher throws another ball and the count goes to 2 and 0, it's time to hit the ball. The pitcher needs to throw a strike, and it's likely going to be a pitch that you can hit so get ready—he doesn't want to go to 3 and 0. If it's a curve, wait on it and drive the ball through the infielders for a base hit. If it's a fastball, take a good cut and hit the ball hard. Always try to get ahead on the count; it puts pressure on the pitcher to throw a strike. The farther the pitcher gets ahead in the count, the harder the pitches will be to hit. There are really two types of hitters. There is the defensive hitter who stands at the plate and reads the pitch and decides if he's going to swing. Then there is the offensive type of hitter that every pitch is a strike and he's going to start his swing and hold up if it's a bad pitch. After starting his swing and he then sees it's a bad pitch, he holds up or check swings. The offensive hitter tries to hit every pitch and the defensive watches them until he sees a good pitch. We really never know what the pitch is going to be, but if we see a pitcher enough and narrow down what he does in certain situations and what type of pitches he throws, it may give you a little more confidence at the plate when it's our turn to face him. The real key is who's ahead in the count and when is it time for a pitch you can hit.

Chapter 6
Playing the Infield

The Infielders

The Infielders

The infielders are a unique group of players that hold down the offense generated by the opposing team. I look for certain attributes from infield players who play the different positions. The first baseman is normally tall in the event one of the other players makes a bad throw over his head and he must reach for the ball or he must scoop a one hopper out of the dirt by doing the splits. Some coaches have the mindset that the first baseman needs to be left-handed to help make defensive throws in the infield. I don't think that's always true in some cases. I see first basemen as confident and strong players demonstrating a solid character on and off the field. You don't necessarily need to be left-handed, but it helps. First, because of their size, first basemen are power hitters and drive in runs by batting three or four in the lineup. The second baseman is smaller in stature and able to turn double plays quickly. He plays with poise and consistency on a daily basis. His eyes and head are always in the game looking for someone to get out. Second basemen are very skilled with catching ground balls, pivoting during double plays, and good at throwing on the run. They make good leadoff hitters because of their consistency in hitting the ball and their speed on the bases. I usually place them batting 1 or 2. The shortstop can do it all. He is our best infielder and has the natural ability to play the ball and throw runners out from the edge of the infield grass. Shortstops come in all sizes, but most are medium height with very strong throwing arms. They have the ability to throw a rocket to first and relay strong throws from the outfield to home plate to the catcher. Shortstops love to compete and are great hitters and base stealers. Last we have the third baseman. Playing third base takes a player that has no fear catching a line drive or a hard-hit ground ball down the left-field line. The third baseman is just plain tough and challenges the hitter to hit the ball to him. He loves to play in-your-face baseball and charge a bunt. He throws on a line from third to first with pinpoint accuracy and loves to field the ball on the run and deliver it to first base. He is a power hitter that should hit 3 or 4 in the lineup. He loves to steal and is one of the most aggressive players on the baseball team.

The Catcher

The Catcher

The catcher is one of the toughest and most important parts of a good defensive baseball team. He is the commander in chief on all defensive plays. This makes perfect sense because he sits behind the plate and has a full view of the baseball field, enabling him to take charge and let everyone know where the baseball is being thrown. It's also the catcher who gives defensive signals to defend against opposing teams' base runners during a first and third situation or attempted bunted ball. The catcher must also give signals to the pitcher, indicating which pitch should be thrown while at the same time helping him stay calm and focused. There's no question the catcher's arm needs to be strong and accurate to throw out base runners. His ability should be demonstrated during pregame warm-ups and throughout the entire game. This will show the opposing team his ability to make defensive plays and throw out base runners who try to steal a base. It's also the catcher's job to study the other team's lineup to take advantage of their hitting weaknesses and ability to steal bases. Having the quickness to move up, down, and side to side to block pitches is a must. Wearing protective gear that is comfortable and allows him to move quickly and throw the ball without being restricted is important. Catchers are smart about when and where they throw the baseball as well as being tough, solid defensive players that demonstrate a competitive nature. They build solid relationships with the players and coaches. It's not easy being a great catcher who displays the right kind of leadership to win games, but the rewards are well worth it.

Chest High Throws Drill!

2000 World Series Champions

New York Yankees 4-1

2001 World Series Champions

Arizona Diamondbacks 4-3

2002 World Series Champions

Anaheim Angels 4-3

2003 Worls Series Champions

Florida Marlins 4-2

2004 World Series Champions

Boston Red Sox 4-0

Chest-High Throw Drill

When I started coaching, I watched the younger players having trouble throwing the baseball and hitting their target. They would work hard to catch a hard-hit ground ball and then make a wild throw, the wild throws turned into the runners advancing and runs being scored. As a coach, I wanted to come up with a solution for the wild throws and missed opportunities. When I talked to the team, I expressed that we needed to improve our throws and hit our targets in the chest when throwing the baseball. I told them I was implemented a new drill to eliminate the wild throws. The drill went like this: I had the players form two single files, one player behind the other facing each others back. The first player in each line would step out to the side of their line. The players were about thirty feet apart to start depending on how good I thought they would do. To begin the drill, I would toss the ball to a player who would then throw the ball chest high to the player waiting thirty feet away who would catch the ball and return it with a chest-high throw to a new player who had stepped out. Once the players had thrown the ball, it would be their job to move quickly to get out of the way and go to the end of the line so a new player could step out to catch the next throw. I made sure after players had made their throw, they hustled to the end of the line; there was no walking. The players would throw the ball back and forth, focusing on making perfect throws. I watch every throw, and I always made players chase a wild throw if they missed the target. We did the drill every practice and before games. Once the players had the hang of it, I would speed up the drill, never forgetting the focus on the ball hitting the chest. I also increase the distance of the throws as we improved. Our throws got better, and players began to see how important throwing accurately was to winning games. Our throwing errors went down.

Quick Catch Drill!

2005 World Series Champions

Chicago White Sox 4-0

2006 World Series Champions

St. Louis Cardinals 4-1

2007 World Series Champions

Boston Red Sox 4-0

2008 World Series Champions

Philadelphia Phillies 4-1

Quick-Catch Drill

After spending time with our chest-high throws, the players stay in their lines, and we would jump into our quick catch drill. Quick catch is an important drill to teach players to find the baseball in their gloves and get rid of it quickly. It doesn't matter what position you play finding the baseball, and getting rid of it quickly is essential to playing good defense. Quick catch helps teams turn double plays and send an important message to the other team that you are a skilled fielder. Quick-catch drill is performed just like chest-high throws, only the players catch the ball and release it quickly. We always made sure our players were paying attention during this drill; sometimes the throws and catches get a little sloppy. It was important to me to put the players in lines; I wanted to watch every player pushing them to find the ball in their glove and get rid of it.

Quick-Tag

And

Show-the-Umpire-the-Ball Drill

2009 World Series Champions

New York Yankees 4-2

2010 World Series Champions

San Francisco Giants 4-1

2011 World Series Champions

St. Louis Cardinals 4-3

2012 World Series Champions

San Francisco Giants 4-0

Quick-Tag and Show-the-Umpire-the-Ball Drill

After quick catch, we move right into quick tag and show the baseball. We used the same lines and same execution for catching the ball then tagging the runner and showing the ball to the umpire. Quick tag is performed so the runner won't try to dislodge the ball from the defensive player's glove and the quick tag helps the umpire make the right call when a player is sliding into a base. We would throw the ball back and forth quick tagging until we looked smooth and consistent catching, tagging, and showing the ball to the umpire. Remember, in all these drills, we always stepped to the ball and centered it while moving forward so it was on our throwing side.

PLAY THE HOP
DON'T LET THE BALL
PLAY YOU!

2013 World Series Champions

Boston Red Sox 4-2

2014 World Series Champions

San Francisco Giants 4-3

2015 World Series Champions

Kansas city Royals 4-1

2016 World Series Champions

Chicago Cubs 4-3

One Hop Drill!

2017 World Series Champions

Houston Astros 4-3

2018 World Series Champions

Boston Red Sox 4-1

2019 World Series Champions

Washington Nationals 4-3

2020 World Series Champions

Los Angeles Dodgers 4-2

One-Hop Drill

One-hop drill is performed to help players decide when and how to catch the hop. The idea is to field the baseball (short hop) right after it hits the ground or (long hop) when the baseball has traveled to its highest point during the hop. Knowing how to play the hop gives the player the ability to time an approaching ball that's going to hop. Being able to play the hop gives you added confidence when fielding the tough baseballs. By performing this drill, the players would once again stay in their lines and throw short hops to the other player waiting to play it. Each player would field the ball and throw it back short hopping to the next player who stepped out from the line. After a few minutes, we would be back and throw long hops, working on catching the ball at its highest point. This drill might be ugly at first. Make sure you give it time; it's a great drill. If you're having trouble with the hops, you might want to practice this drill on the pavement at first.

Center The Ball Drill!

2021 World Series Champions

Atlanta Braves 4-2

Centering the Ball Drill

Centering the ball drill is practiced to help the players move their bodies to a position where they catch the ball on their throwing side while moving forward and then throwing it without having to pivot. To practice the drill, players should pair up and face each other in two lines twenty-five to thirty feet apart, leaving ten feet of spacing between players. The players would throw the baseball back and forth, stepping to the ball to position themselves to receive the ball on their throwing side. Once they've caught the ball, they would continue forward getting under control and throwing the ball off your front leg. Like any drill, it might feel strange at first, but as you get the hang of it, you'll realize the drill's importance.

Throw the Ball Firm, No Soft Throws In Baseball!

Throw the Ball Firm, No Soft Throws in Baseball!

Always remember, no soft throws in baseball. I've always taught players to flip the ball underhand on a close play; not hard, but firm, and deliver it underhand, making sure you show the baseball when releasing it. Throwing a baseball hard overhand at a short distance handcuffs the receiving player's ability to judge the throw and see the ball. When a player is too far away to flip the ball, then the firm overhand toss becomes appropriate to make the play. I still insist on the short overhand toss that the player show the ball and throw it firmly. Players must learn when and how hard to throw a baseball to make solid defensive plays. Sometimes players will catch a hard-hit ground ball, relax too much, then throw the ball too soft, making it go wild or short for the other player to catch. When this happens, the throw becomes a short hop, making the receiving player scoop the ball or on a high throw, causing missed catch for an easy out. Don't let up on your throws. Know what kind of throw is needed to make the play. Firm throws make plays; soft throws cause errors.

<u>Make Eye Contact With The Player You're Throwing The Ball Too!</u>

Make Eye Contact With The Player You're Throwing

The Ball Too! Making eye contact with the player you're throwing the ball to is more for safety than anything else. When I was young and starting out as a new coach, I was around a lot of very young players that would hit someone with the baseball because the other player wasn't looking. I use a simple rule that saves a lot of injuries and headaches. If you don't have eye contact with the player you're throwing the ball to, don't throw it. If you're a coach and players only hear you say this rule one time, it won't be enough; say it over and over, especially with the younger players, and it will catch on. Don't throw the ball unless you have eye contact. It's a good rule! Keep your head in the game, know what's going on around you and where the baseball is being thrown. Players who relax for a moment and think the play is over find out that's when they get hit.

Charge the Ball!

Charge the Ball!

Charging the baseball at a young age is important. It helps shorten up throws on infield plays and get the ball back to the pitcher quickly from the outfield. It's important when charging ground balls to give yourself time to sit down on the ball to catch it clean. I've always thought charging a grounder teaches young players to be aggressive and sends a message that your playing the ball, the ball not playing you. Watching players approaching ground balls it's easy to see timing is everything when the ball takes a hop. Whether you decide to catch the ball at the height of its bounce or you decide to scoop it off the ground, it's all about timing. After the catch always come up under control and gather yourself to make a perfect throw. The older the player, the fewer opportunities there will be to charge a ground ball. It's simple—older players hit the ball harder. I always look for aggressive players that take charge getting to the ball then demonstrating good timing and accurate throws.

Scoop Pause
And Throw!

Scoop Pause and Throw!

The word _scoop_ was a catchy way of reminding my players to catch a ground ball out in front, sitting down on it instead of bending over. Sitting down on the ball and keeping your glove out in front prevents the ball from passing through your legs while blocking it and giving you the opportunity to still make the play. _Pause_ was to get players to get their bodies under control and come up smooth after the catch. _Throw_ was finding their target, making eye contact, and delivering the throw accurately. We have all witnessed a hurried catch and throw, causing the best players to chuck the ball up into the cheap seats. When a player catches a ground ball, remember to sit down on it then scope, pause, and throw. Even when catching a fly ball in the outfield, the outfielder should catch, pause, and then throw. It also helps if a fielder centers himself during the catch and lines himself up in the direction of his throw. If the fielder is driven backward on the catch, they need to stop and get their bodies moving in the right direction toward their target before throwing. Catchers are a good example of getting in position to throw the ball correctly. We've all witnessed the ball ending up out front of the plate and the catcher jumping out, circulating the ball, ending up facing his target before he throws. It's a good example of aligning yourself to make a good throw while under control.

____

____

____

____

Walk Up on the Pitch!

Walk Up on the Pitch!

There are a lot of different names for walking up on a pitch, such as creeping, moving, or sneaking. Whatever name your coach uses is meant for one purpose—to move all his fielders in one direction toward the plate as the pitch is being thrown. He wants his players moving and ready. The walk up keeps players from setting back on their heels or standing flat-footed. Players who aren't moving have a slower reaction time when making a catch or defensive play. When the pitcher delivers the pitch, infielders as well as outfielders should be walking forward with their glove and palm open toward the hitter. As they walk forward, their knees are slightly bent, their glove out in front and open, ready to respond to a hit. Physics teaches us that it takes less time for your body to react if it's already moving. The walk up before the pitch is three simple steps right, left, right. It's just the opposite if you're left-handed, left, right, left. Outfielders as well as infielders should all be moving at the same time in unison as the pitch is delivered. Smart players will watch the ball as it's thrown to see whether the pitch is inside, outside, low, or high and then adjust their walk up to where they think the ball is going to be hit. I've always felt being an aggressive player, and walking up on the pitch gives a slight edge and builds confidence in players to make great plays. Remember, the walk up is to get your body moving and ready to make plays.

Make Sure

of the First One!

Make Sure of the First One!

We've all heard the coach say make sure of the first one when turning the double play. He knows the problems that can occur if players try to turn the play too fast; they end up making mistakes and losing outs. Turning a good double play takes lots of practice and good execution between players. Knowing where to place the ball in the bag at the correct moment helps the next player catch it and get rid of it quickly. Whether you're flipping or tossing the ball, it must be accurate and playable if the double play is going to be successful. On a toss or flip, make sure you show the ball and try not to rise up while getting rid of it. If you rise up, the ball will come up and make it harder to handle.

The Rundown!

The Rundown!

Once in a while, a base runner will be too aggressive and try to steal or advance on the bases and get caught in a rundown. The first thing to remember in a rundown situation is to always throw the baseball ahead of the base runner and run him back to the base he came from. When running him down or back to the base he came from, you should show the ball by holding it up with your throwing hand so the runner and the other fielders can see the ball. During the rundown when you're holding the ball up, fake a couple of throws to the other fielder waiting on the base to trick the base runner. Then when you do attempt to throw the ball to the fielder covering the base, make sure you don't handcuff him with a throw that is too hard to handle. In most rundowns, there needs to be only one throw to the bag for the tag. If too many throws go back and forth too many times, there's a good chance someone will miss the catch or drop the ball. If you have the ball, hold it up, run the base runner down, and make one throw to the fielder on the bag to tag the runner out. The fielder on base waiting for the throw should call out now when he wants the ball for the tag. If the base runner ends up safe, remember he's back where he's started and nothing has been lost. When there's a rundown between first and second, the pitcher helps the first baseman if he needs to come off the bag and goes after the base runner with the ball. At that time the pitcher will take over the base and be ready if they come back his way. The shortstop helps the second baseman in the same manner. If the second baseman goes after the base runner the shortstop takes over second base ready in case they come back his way. Whoever has the ball and makes a throw should keep going to the opposite base ready to help if the base runner comes back their way. If the rundown is between second and third then the pitcher backs up third base. If the third baseman leaves his bag to chase down the base runner, then the pitcher takes over the bag. Shortstop helps the second baseman in the same way, taking over second base if needed. It's important in practice to simulate rundown situations so players know what to do and feel confident.

Chapter 7

Outfield Play

Outfielders

Field the Ball Clean

Outfielders Field the Ball Clean

Why is it so important to catch outfield grounders clean? During games, smart base runners look for bobbled catches so they can take an extra base. They also know that if the ball is misplayed by the outfielder, it throws his timing off, and he has trouble getting rid of the ball quickly. The outfielder will hurry his throw and miss the cutoff man or make a wild throw to base and miss the tag. When playing a hard-hit ground ball, catch it out in front with your feet shoulder-width apart. When the ball comes, sit down on it, making sure your glove's out in front. If you make the mistake of bending over rather than sitting down the ball could go through your legs because your butt was too high and the tip of your glove is to high. If it's a do-or-die situation, play the ball off the ground while on the run, staying low and coming up after the catch then throwing off your front foot. When playing a baseball that's taking a big hop, catch it at the high point of the hop or on the short hop just when it hits the ground. Try not to catch the baseball in the middle of its hop to keep it from handcuffing you. It's always easier to catch the ball at the top of its flight or just after it hits the ground to take away the angle of it coming up. When the ball hits the ground and starts upward, it can be hard to make a clean catch and get rid of it quickly. Catching the ball clean is important to keep runners honest and let them know that you're ready if they try to stretch a single into a double.

Get Rid of the Ball!

Get Rid of the Ball!

Always get rid of the ball. Get it back to the pitcher if there's not going to be another play. Taking your time holding on to the ball will cost you runs. Players will steal bases and cause disruption in the game. After catching the ball, GET RID OF IT!

<u>Hit the Relay Man!</u>

Hit the Relay Man!

Hitting the relay man from the outfield is imperative and one of the keys for playing good defense. Coaches know that good outfield play holds base runners up from running the bases as well as helping to throw runners out at home. When the ball is hit to the outfield, it's important the defensive player field the ball clean and throw it quickly to the relay man who gets the ball back into the infield to stop base runners from advancing. The quicker you can get the ball back to the infield, the less likely base runners will attempt to score. It's the job of the second baseman or shortstop to go out and set up as a relay between the outfielder who is fielding the ball and where the ball is to be thrown. If the ball is hit to left field, the shortstop goes out for the relay; and if it's hit to right field, the second baseman will go out as the relay man. The relay man makes himself a big target calling for the ball, making sure the outfielder knows where to throw. Once the outfielder's relay throw is on the way, the relay judges the ball then turns his body to catch the ball on his throwing side. Positioning himself before the ball arrives saves time by not having to pivot after the catch and sets his body up to throw the ball quickly. Hitting the relay man with a chest-high throw from the outfield saves time and helps the relay process become smooth and quick. After catching the throw, the relay man can make a play on a base runner. If there's no play, he simply runs the ball back into the infield and tosses it back to the pitcher. On shorter hits to the outfield, the outfielder fielding might decide to make a play, throwing directly to a base or home plate without involving the relay at all. When there's a ball hit long to right field and a base runner is trying to score from second, the first baseman will come off his bag, align himself between the first base bag, and the pitcher's mound to cut off a bad throw to home. If it's a bad throw, the catcher yells to the first baseman to cut the ball and throw to home or to another base. If the ball is hit to center field, once again it's the first baseman's job to become the relay man, aligning himself for the throw to home and listening to the catcher's commands where to throw the ball. If the catcher doesn't yell cut, the first baseman lets the ball go through to the catcher so he can make a play at the plate. If the ball is hit to left field, it's the third baseman's job to come off his bag and become the relay, positioning himself between third base and the pitcher's mound in case of a bad throw. He listens for the catcher's command to move right or left for alignment and whether or not to cut the ball and where to throw it to another base. Once again if he doesn't hear the catcher yell cut, he lets the ball go through so the catcher can make a play at the plate. During the relay process, the pitcher would cover third base on a hit to left field; and on a hit to right, he would back up the catcher.

Catch Fly Balls with Two Hands!

Catch Fly Balls with Two Hands!

Outfielders as well as infielders should always catch fly balls with two hands, especially if no one is on base. When catching a fly ball, pause for a moment and don't be so quick to drop your glove down. I've seen players catch an easy fly ball drop their glove down and the ball falls out, sending a confusing message to the umpire. It can look like you dropped the ball, and umpires will call the runner safe. It only happens once in a great while, so if no base runners are on base, hold your glove up for a moment just to be sure the ball doesn't drop out. If you're running and need to dive to make the catch or it's going to be a fly ball over your head, all bets are off; catch it any way you can. If you know the ball is going over your head, drop step with your foot that's in the direction of the fly ball to help cover more ground quickly. If possible, circle the ball, getting behind it so your running motion is coming forward and you have a stronger throw off your front leg. Remember, when you catch a fly ball with runners on base, know where the ball is going ahead of time then get rid of it. If you're in the outfield, get the ball back quickly to the infield. Hit the cutoff man chest high. If you're an infielder and you catch a fly ball, once again know in advance where you're going to throw the ball. A simple rule after making a catch in the infield is to look for another out. Let the other team see that you're always looking for someone else to get out. After making a catch and there are no other plays, then run the ball into the pitcher, shorting your distance before throwing it to him. Remember, if a fly ball is hit foul and you make the catch, base runners are allowed to tag up and advance; be ready if a runner tries to take a base. Lastly, make sure you understand the chain of command, catching fly balls in the infield and outfield. It goes like this: the center fielder has authority over the left fielder and right fielder when calling a fly ball. All outfielders have authority over infielders on a fly ball. The shortstop has authority over the third baseman while the second baseman has authority over the first baseman and then the first baseman and third baseman have authority over the pitcher who has authority over the catcher. You can see that the chain of command on a fly ball starts in the outfield and works its way into the catcher. It's very important that when a fly ball is hit in a player's direction, he always needs to call it out. If the ball is hit between two players, you might hear both players call out the ball; but by the time the ball is called three times, the chain of command should take over and the right player should know to catch the ball. Communication between players is the key to good defense. A fly ball should be called three times using the words "GET OUT, GET OUT," pause, then one final "GET OUT" by the player that's going to catch the ball. When calling a fly ball, it must be loud to make sure other players know who's in charge and will make the catch. To have a good defense, communication on fly balls should be practiced on a regular basis.

Chapter 8

Team Management

Team Management

Team management on and off the field is one of the keys to having a great baseball program. How your team acts off the field is just as important as there performance on the field. Most teams show great class when competing and representing their community when playing away from home. Sadly I'm sure we've all witnessed teams who have left the visited site after playing and earned the title of being unorganized. Taking a look at how you act on the field is worth discussion. Here are some thoughts concerning managing your team on and off the field which talk about the appearance of your baseball field, transportation of your players, team rules and communication with parents.

The Appearance of The Baseball Field

To me it's real simple, good baseball coaches take care of their field. When I drive down the road and look at the different baseball fields I can tell by their appearance how the baseball program is doing. It's not an easy job keeping the baseball field looking nice. Coaches in most programs assign players the responsibility to help maintain the field. For example the catcher will take care of the plate making sure the batters box is raked and ready for the next practice or game. The rest of the infielders take care of their positions while the pitchers spend time preparing mound making sure it's raked and looking good. The pitchers are also responsible for taking care of the bull pins. Outfielders are assigned the dugout's keeping both the home and visitor's clean by sweeping them out and picking up trash and then putting the baseball equipment away in it's proper storage. I always had older senior players assingned to water and drag the field. It doesn't stop their coaches spend time doing other jobs to make sure the field looks well and funtions like it should. It's all done to set an example and teach players to love baseball and maintain a high standard for the love of the game.

Transportation of Players to Away Games

Rules for transporting players to away games is important for safety and peace off mind of parents and players. During the school year players are transported by school buses to help reduce the problems of being on the road. Most school districts will require coaches to turn in a travel list to the main office. This list will indicate the players and coaches on the bus traveling to the away contest. The coach will also have a medical file of each players emergency information that is important if needed. After the contest is over players should ride back to school on the bus unless a parent request their child be released to them at the game sight. During summer baseball the coaches resposibility begins when players arrive at the baseball field to attend an away game. In most cases older players will drive themselves directly to the away game or the parents will drive their player.

Team Rules and Communication with Parents

Before the seaon begins it's important that coaches set up a parent meeting to go over team rules and requirements for their son to participate. The team rules should be handed out and gone over and then signed by the parents and players. Coaches should talk about player behavior and attendance during the baseball season, appearance, and maintaining their grades during school.

Acknowledgments

I want to thank all my fellow coaches who were apart of my baseball coaching experiences throughtout my life. I would also like to pay tribute to the hundreds of young athletes who have played or been apart of my baseball programs over the years.

To my Grandsons Landon and Logan Sherman thank you for making your grandfather so very proud. Logan it was fun to watch you play baseball. I'm so proud of your efforts on the field. This book is dedicated to you and your great ability to hit the ball and eat pizza. I'm just as proud of all my grandchildren for their ability to care about people and lift everyone up with their wonderful personalities.

To my son in-law Mark, thank you for the many coversations we've had over the years about baseball and for being such a good father. To my daughters Kristyn and Heather you are the love of my life. I know you both will remember all the shortcuts Dad took to get to the baseball games on time.

Thank you to my wonderful wife Christi who listens to all my answers to life's problems using examples from coaching philosophies.